HOW TO BUILD RELATIONSHIPS AND GET JOB OFFERS USING LINKEDIN
First Edition

Written by Robbie Abed

Copyright © 2018 FMIBY

All rights reserved. No part of this book may be utilized, copied or reproduced in any way or form or by any means, electronic or mechanical, including recording and photocopying, or by any retrieval system and information storage without written permission of FMIBY. The only exception is a reviewer, who may quote short excerpts in a review.

ISBN 978-0-692-15430-4

HOW TO BUILD RELATIONSHIPS AND GET JOB OFFERS USING LINKEDIN

ROBBIE ABED

1

TO MY DAUGHTER, DANYA

You have at least one book in you. Dig deep.
Don't Google how many pages a book needs to be.
It doesn't matter.
You will know when it's finished.
And don't ask for cover design feedback on Facebook.
You will end up questioning the meaning of life.
Oh, sorry. Facebook is this thing we used to all be on.
Anyway.
Just do you.

INTRODUCTION

Hi.

I don't believe we've met before.

My name is Robbie.

Robbie is a great name until you're about nine years old.

After nine years old, it's hard to get anyone to take you seriously with a name that belongs to a child.

But, I digress.

The purpose of this book is to give you real insight on the best way to use LinkedIn.

There are hundreds of books and articles about how to use LinkedIn. Most of the books come from resume experts, LinkedIn experts, and copywriters who have more certifications than I'll ever have.

I paid for every single LinkedIn book on Amazon and read every LinkedIn article imaginable. They all say similar things:

1. Optimize your LinkedIn profile, so you show up in recruiter searches.

2. Use a beautiful headshot.

3. Use special characters like ✔ to stand out.

I decided to do something a little different.

Instead of covering every aspect of LinkedIn, I'm going to focus on the few areas you care about: building relationships, getting noticed, and getting job offers.

This book has two major sections:

1. Perspective Changing Concepts

2. LinkedIn Tactics That Work

The tactics section doesn't work if you don't understand the concept of how to effectively use LinkedIn.

I only ask that you open your mind to changing how you feel about LinkedIn. I purposely repeat some concepts to drive a few points home.

I'm hoping the repetition will trigger an "Ahh, this guy is on to something!" moment.

The tactics I mention are effective. You're not going to learn about some secret LinkedIn hack that only a few people know. However, you will learn that with the right discipline, you will see a big difference in the effectiveness of LinkedIn for your career or business.

Let's start with nine perspective changing concepts!

PART I

9 PERSPECTIVE CHANGING CONCEPTS

#1- The Actual Interview Doesn't Happen During the Interview.

I received a random LinkedIn message from a college friend. Her company was hiring, and she thought I would be a great fit. She introduced me to the Senior Vice President (SVP) of the division. I had one informal phone interview, and he invited me to attend the once-a-year company party and also interview with other people in his group.

I was the only person invited to the party who didn't work at the company. The people I had interviewed with the day before were astonished that I was invited.

"How did you get invited to the company party? You don't even work here yet? I'm not even sure why I'm interviewing you."

I still remember when one of my interviewers told this to me. I had the job in the bag before the formal interviews even began.

All I needed was the SVP to give his blessing, and the rest was downhill. Keep in mind, HR and Recruiting have no idea I even exist. I submitted my resume as a formality after our interviews were complete.

I proceeded to have a blast at the party and met everyone I would potentially work with.

Now, I'm not telling you this to brag. I'm telling this to you so you understand that you don't have to follow the traditional hiring system to go through the process. The faster you can get an SVP to endorse you for a job, the easier everything becomes.

Read this little quip from the former SVP of People at Google:

"In other words, most interviews are a waste of time because 99.4 percent of the time is spent trying to confirm whatever impression the interviewer formed in the first ten seconds. 'Tell me about yourself.' 'What is your greatest weakness?' 'What is your greatest strength?' Worthless."

If you're like me, you're probably the worst first impression maker of all time.

So, if 99.4% of the time the interview is a waste of time because they are too busy confirming their bias, what do you do?

You make the first impression before you speak to them.

Here's how I used LinkedIn to make a great first impression and bypass the traditional hiring system.

I wrote about productivity and project management on LinkedIn. My friend, whom I haven't spoken to in 4 years, loved my articles and thought I would be a good fit for their growing company. She also had a great relationship with the SVP.

The productivity post had over 400,000 views, and that was social proof that I knew what I was doing.

That's all the SVP needed to hear. Our phone interview was less than 15 minutes before he invited me to the company party.

Social Proof Makes Every Interview a Breeze.

I never got asked, "What's your greatest strength?" You know why? They already knew what my greatest strength was. They already read my articles on productivity and project management on LinkedIn. They saw all the comments on the articles. They already read my LinkedIn profile which laid out clearly why someone would hire me.

So, when I walked into my first formal on-site interview, it was immediately a friendly conversation instead of a formal question and answer interview I was expecting. The SVP already told the interviewers that he liked me. The deal was done before I arrived.

What does this mean for you?

You have to work on building social proof and make sure your online presence tells everyone what you're good at. If the interviewers don't know anything about you during your first interview, you lost. You made your life that much more challenging.

When you interview or apply for a job, the interviewer gets as much information about you as possible. Your resume, LinkedIn profile, Social Media, and Google.

Let that sink in. Before you even utter a word to a real person, they have already formed a judgment of you. If you use LinkedIn the effective way, you will change how others think of you.

It's the difference between getting an unsolicited opportunity or nothing at all.

#2- It's Not the Medium. It's the Message.

If you've been on LinkedIn long enough, you'll notice the platform changes every so often. In late 2014, LinkedIn focused on long-form posts, also known as "LinkedIn

Pulse." When the Pulse platform launched, I was lucky enough to be an early contributor.

This article had close to 500,000 views, which is incredible.

As of mid-2018, it's clear that LinkedIn is pushing users to more short-form posts.

Robbie Abed
Author, Ghostwriter, Marketer, Executive Branding Coach
6d · Edited

I created an extensive step by step guide to building relationships, getting noticed & getting job offers using LinkedIn. It requires action, but it works really well.

If you want a free copy, please comment with "Interested" and also add me as a connection. I'll send it later next week.

EDIT: Well, the response is a little more than I can handle. Type "interested" and fill out this form. https://lnkd.in/gzYXP-d

(Feel free to add me as well)

170 Likes · 526 Comments

👍 Like   💬 Comment   ↗ Share

📈 **112,376 views** of your post in the feed

When I wrote the above status message, I was hoping I would get 20 comments. Instead, I received over 500 comments and over 110,000+ views at the time I wrote this book.

Do you know why these posts spread like wildfire? They spread because I hit a massive pain point with the LinkedIn community. Yes, it helps that I have a large network, but I would estimate 60-70% of the engagement on that post came from 2nd and 3rd degree connections.

Which brings me to your first perspective changing lesson. **If you genuinely understand the pain point of your clients, colleagues, and hiring managers, you will see success on the LinkedIn platform.**

Don't get caught up in the exact tactics and word-for-word scripts that so many marketers offer. Focus on what your message is. **If your message resonates with your connections, you will see more success.**

As long as you have a minimum of 500+ connections on LinkedIn, any of your status messages can be far reaching, especially if your message resonates with your audience. You can't force something to go viral. It doesn't work like that.

If done properly, you will get better response rates to your inMails. You will get more engagement on your statuses and articles. You will get more people that will see you in real life and say, "Hey, I saw what you wrote on LinkedIn. I agree with you."

#3- Interesting Original Content Gets Interesting People Interested In You.

After you finish reading this tongue twister of a title, check out a screenshot of the latest three people to add me on LinkedIn:

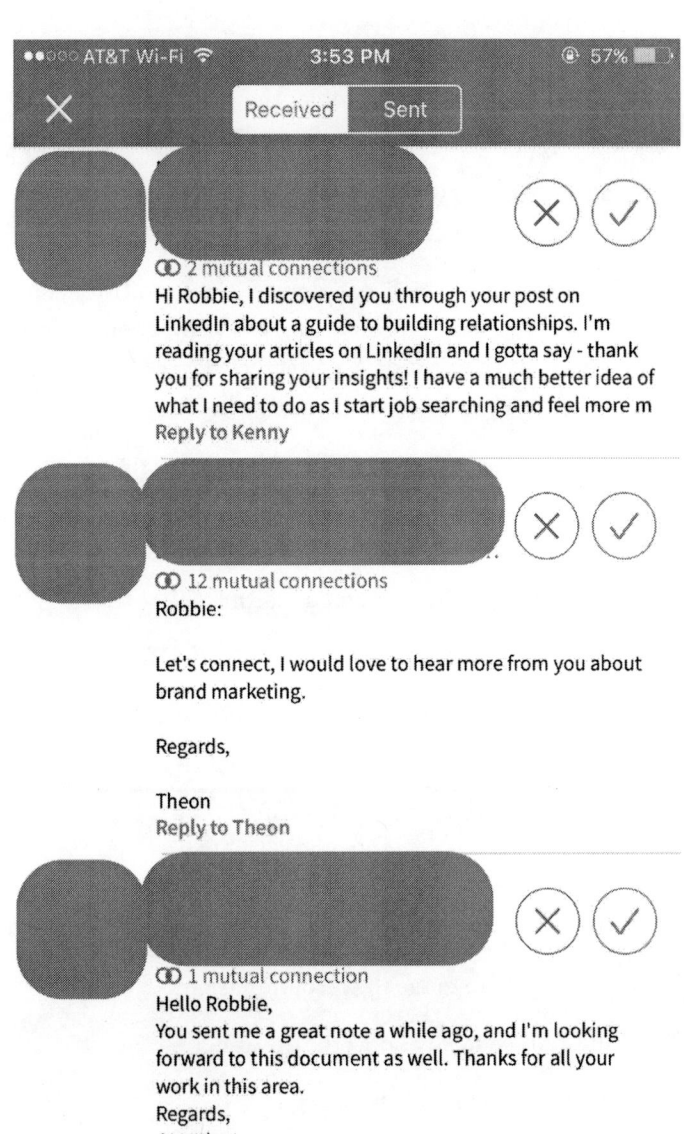

To be noticed you must create original content that

teaches others new things. I've noticed if you can change someone's perspective on a topic, they will become a life long fan.

Are you creating new content? Most people are afraid to write. Don't overthink it. Talk about what you know.

Imagine you're in a small conference room, and someone says to you "Lisa - tell me everything you know about how to run a successful project as a project manager." Do you sit there and stare at him until everyone walks away?

Share your knowledge. Others will appreciate it. Stop worrying about if you're a good writer or not. If you know what you're talking about, it will be appreciated.

It's called a SOCIAL network for a reason!

#4- Social Proof Will Get You Noticed More Often.

Have you ever walked by a restaurant and seen a huge line out the door?

After you saw the line, what did you do?

Did you:

A) Ignore it and keep walking?

B) Stop and look up to see the restaurant sign?

Trick question. I already know the answer.

Only psychopaths keep walking.

Everyone else stops and thinks, "What's going on here? What kind of restaurant is this? It must be popular! I need to learn more. If everyone else loves this place, I might like it too!"

The long line is "social proof" in action.

Hell, you weren't even looking for a restaurant! You were just trying to mind your own business, and this freaking restaurant with a line out the door piqued your interest.

Well, to be fair, the restaurant didn't pique your interest. **The line did.**

Let's take a look at the definition of social proof on Wikipedia:

"Social proof is a type of conformity. When a person is in a situation where they are unsure of the correct way to behave, they will often look to others for cues concerning the correct behavior. "

So, what in the world does this have to do with LinkedIn?

The reason you are reading this book in the first place is that you want to get noticed more. We all know getting noticed is hard, if not damn near impossible.

However, the real problem isn't about getting noticed. It's all about engagement. You don't want someone to see your profile and not engage with it. You want your connections to comment, like, share your posts, and preferably reach out to you with an opportunity.

Engagement is a 3 step process:

1. Get noticed (you show up in their feed)
2. Get them interested (they click on your profile)
3. Engage with you (they reach out to you via inMail, add you as a connection, engage with your posts, etc.)

The issue is that many of you have a restaurant with great food, except there is never a queue out your door. The "psychopaths" just keep walking by.

Social proof comes in many forms on LinkedIn.

Here are some social proof indicators when looking at someone's profile on LinkedIn:

1. They have more than 500 connections.
2. All status posts have high engagement.
3. Long form articles have a lot of likes and comments.
4. Created content that shows they know their subject expertise.
5. Connections that engage with their content frequently.
6. A lot of profile recommendations from current and previous colleagues.
7. They have been mentioned in other industry publications outside of LinkedIn.
8. Worked or works for a recognizable brand name company.

How many of the above social proof indicators can you confidently say that you have? If it's less than 50%, you have a problem.

Let's do a little exercise. I want you to look at your LinkedIn profile from another perspective. Imagine you never met yourself and now you're seeing yourself for the first time.

I could argue that you don't know who you really are in the first place, but that's for another book!

The entire point of this chapter is to make sure you know one thing:

Social proof will increase your chances of getting high engagement. Just being good at what you do isn't enough, unfortunately.

Do you know why I included the screen shots of my high trafficked posts and engagement early in this book as opposed to later?

I did it for social proof. I know that if you see my success, you're more likely to believe what I write for the rest of this book. I'm not an egomaniac, believe it or not.

Take an outside look at your profile and your activity on LinkedIn.

Stop being the restaurant with great food that doesn't have a line out the door.

#5- Show me First. Tell me Second.

When someone tells me they are great at something like Instagram marketing, the first thing I do is look at their Instagram profile or their company's Instagram. If they have less than 100 followers, then something is off. In this instance, they don't have social proof, and it's an immediate turn-off.

The same applies to you. Employers care where you've worked and what your duties were, but they also want to see the quality of your work.

- If you're a programmer, they'll ask you to show them what you've created.
- If you're an editor, they'll ask you to show them the

before and after of an article you've edited.
- If you're a marketer, they'll ask you to show them a marketing plan you've created and the results it got.
- If you're a designer, they'll ask you to show them your portfolio.
- If you're an accountant, they'll ask you to show them what you did to help people save thousands of dollars on their tax returns every year.
- If you're a lawyer, they'll ask you to show them what laws are working against them and how you can better structure their company to avoid such things.

Show employers that you know what you're talking about — that's the bottom line of what potential employers are looking for today. It also happens to be the core problem with resumes. They're all about telling and not showing.

It's like we're in elementary school and doing a show and tell. Can you imagine if it was just "tell"? That would be pointless.

Show me first, tell me second.

LinkedIn gives you all of the tools to do it. You have no excuses.

#6- Long Time Listener, First Time Caller.

Have you ever listened to a radio show, and the caller goes, "Long time listener, first time caller!"

This means the caller has been listening to the show for years but never called the radio station to ask a question or make a comment.

The caller knows everything about the show. They listen to

it every morning. But, they haven't engaged the radio DJ's one bit.

How often have you called a radio show? I don't think I've ever called a radio station in my life.

What does this have to do with getting noticed on LinkedIn?

Just because you don't get likes, shares, or comments, doesn't mean people aren't listening to you or don't like what you're saying.

This point is probably the hardest one to swallow, even for me. Likes, shares, and comments are what makes the world turn. We're all obsessed with engagement. We like to feel that we're saying things other people agree with.

I know this is a fact because I'll see someone I haven't seen in at least two years and the first thing they'll say to me is that they love reading what I write on LinkedIn. I'm always amazed because they never engaged with anything I wrote.

Don't be discouraged if your engagement is low. Trust me. They are reading what you write. We're all hooked on Facebook and LinkedIn.

So, don't get desperate to write things on LinkedIn just to see if anyone else is out there. Stay on message. **The social proof will come if you're consistent.**

#7- So, What Do You Do Again?

I want you to go on LinkedIn and Facebook. Don't act like you deactivated Facebook. I know you still have it.

Scroll through your news feed as you normally would, except this time I want you to stop at the first five people you see in your feed.

Ask yourself these two questions for each person you see in your feed:

1. "What exactly does this person do?"

2. "What job posting or job opening would trigger me to think of this person as a potential hire?"

Let me guess. You had trouble answering those two questions. Isn't it amazing how little we know?

Now, flip it around and think about how this relates to you. When you pop up in someone's news feed, do they know exactly what you do? If they saw an incredible opportunity come up, would they know enough to reach out to you?

The problem isn't that you don't appear in their newsfeed. Your connections see your name pop up all the time. The problem is that they have no idea what you do or why someone would hire you. That's the REAL issue.

So, the main point is this: Just being on LinkedIn isn't enough. You have to make sure they know exactly what your value proposition is.

How do you do this?

You don't do this by posting political content every day.

You don't do this by posting, "I'm a great project manager" every week. That's just weird.

But if you post status messages and create articles that talk about how to run successful projects, then you're helping others understand what you do for a living, and establishing yourself as someone who is knowledgeable.

That's when you'll start to see success on LinkedIn.

#8- If You Suck in Real Life, You're Going to Suck on LinkedIn.

I don't care if you follow exactly what other successful LinkedIn users do. If you suck in real life, it will be apparent to everyone in the community.

This advice includes everything I've written in this book.

I can't make you better at what you do.

If you want to be noticed on LinkedIn, you have to be an interesting person.

If you have nothing unique to share, you're not an interesting person.

If you aren't actively involved in your industry, you're most likely not an interesting person.

It doesn't matter if I give you a word-for-word email script to send to someone. If you're not interesting, they won't respond back. **There is no formula in the world to get them to respond back to you.**

If Richard Branson sends you a message on LinkedIn that says, "Coffee this Thursday? I want to learn more about what you do."

You're going to respond in .2 seconds and say, "HELL YES!"

If a random person sends you a message with the same exact script, what is your response going to be?

For starters, you're going to ask yourself, "Who the hell are you and what do you want from me?"

This is why most LinkedIn inMail messages and connection requests get ignored.

The person who reached out to you just isn't interesting. They have no social proof, no original viewpoints, and an incomplete profile.

Who you are matters more than the tactics you use. Stop looking for the shortcut to LinkedIn success.

#9- How Do You Keep in Touch With So Many People?

OK, Mr. Popular! You want to know what the best way to stay in touch with everyone you've met and all your amazing LinkedIn connections?

The answer to that question is "You don't and you can't."

But, that's not a good enough answer.

So, I'm going to come through with a perspective-changer for you.

Do you know the best way to keep in touch with 500+ LinkedIn connections?

Create and publish content that you believe in. The more consistently you do it, the better off you are.

Like I said before. Your connections might not engage with you, but trust me when I say that they do read it.

When they feel the opportunity to reach out to you after not speaking to you for a long time, they will have already "kept in touch with you" by reading your LinkedIn posts and articles.

If you reach out to them, it won't be "out of nowhere" because they have been keeping up with you and your content.

That's how you keep in touch with everybody.

PART II

LINKEDIN TACTICS THAT WORK

WHERE THE RUBBER MEETS THE ROAD

OK—You're probably sick of conceptual stuff and want to dive into more specific LinkedIn tactics. Let's do it.

Actually, let's do something a little different. I'm live on air, WBBC 92.1, and someone is calling in. Let's hear what they have to say.

Robbie,

I already see where you're going with this book. You're going to make us create content and do other things that require a lot of action. It's a novel idea, and it probably works.

But, can I be real with you for one second? I don't have the time to do what you're going to recommend. I can MAYBE update my LinkedIn profile based on your recommendations, but anything more than that is going to be tough.

Let's talk about all the things that are going to prevent me from taking action:

1. I hate writing. No, seriously. I hate it. I'm not good at it.
2. I have no time. Even if I made time, someone else will take it from me. I have a demanding job and a family to take care of.
3. I've been taught to not talk about myself. How can I do what you teach and not look like an egomaniac?

Lastly, I just ask one thing from you. Be real with us. We've been to this rodeo before. Don't sugarcoat what it takes to build relationships and get job offers. Don't make it seem easier than it is.

Sincerely,

Confused in Cleveland.

And, oh yeah! Long time listener, first time caller!

Confused in Cleveland,

I love it when random readers call into my nonexistent radio show! Let me be the first one to welcome you to "Coffee with Robbie," where there is no such thing as stupid questions, just stupid people.

Let's break your issues down.

"I hate writing. No, seriously. I hate it. I'm not good at it."

Imagine that your boss just told you to give a presentation on the future of technology in the Insurance Industry.

Are you going to say, "No thanks! I suck at presentations! Find someone else."

No. You're going to do the presentation, and it's going to be great.

You don't hate writing. You do it every day.

Write the way you talk. Write the way you send emails and create presentations.

Start there.

"I have no time. Even if I made time, someone else would take it from me. I have a demanding job and family to take care of."

Don't set yourself on fire to make someone else warm.

You're reading this book because you want to build relationships and get job offers. It's not called, "How to make your company more money."

Get your priorities straight. Take charge of your career before someone else does.

"I've been taught to not talk about myself. How can I do what you teach and not look like I'm showing off?"

Are your teachers and professors egomaniacs?

Every day they get up in front of a classroom and show everyone how smart they are. Isn't that the definition of arrogance?

The difference is that teachers are teaching. You respect anyone that teaches you something new.

If you become a teacher and show everyone what you know, you can stop being afraid of being viewed as a show-off.

Thanks for calling. I have to get back to writing now.

NOW we can dive into the tactics.

LINKEDIN TACTICS THAT WORK

I split up the LinkedIn tactics section into 4 brief, but powerful chapters:

1. Create a LinkedIn profile that doesn't suck
2. How to build new relationships
3. How to get job offers
4. How to get noticed

Create a LinkedIn Profile That Doesn't Suck

I don't usually ask for much.

But, I'm going to ask for something that's probably a lot for a stranger to ask.

I need you to have an out-of-body experience. I need you to pretend you're not in your own body.

You're on the outside looking in.

I'll wait here while you have this experience.

Still waiting.

You there?

Perfect. Here's what I want you to do.

I want your new body to look at your main LinkedIn profile.

Now, ask yourself these two questions:

1. On a scale of 1 to 7, how interesting is this person?
2. Would I want to meet this person to learn more about them?

Be brutally honest.

If it's not at least a 6 out of 7, then you have some work to do.

It could be that you're truly just not an interesting person.

It could also be that your LinkedIn profile sucks.

I'm going to assume it's the latter. Let's fix that right now.

By the way, I rate everything out of 7. It bothers the hell out of everyone. I don't care. All I know is that they will remember for the rest of their lives that Robbie rates things out of 7.

It's different.

So, that's why you're going to focus on creating a LinkedIn profile that's different and, most importantly, memorable.

Step 1: You need to pay for a professional LinkedIn profile picture. No, seriously.

I honestly don't recommend paying for many things. A professional picture is on the top of my list of things to pay for.

Your selfie isn't going to work. That great picture of you that your buddy snapped before you went out on a night on the town isn't going to work. If you didn't pay for it, it most likely shouldn't be your profile picture.

It's the difference between "I want to learn more about this person," and "I have no interest in this person... Next!"

Keep in mind that once you've paid for a great headshot, you can reuse this for your own personal blog or publications, for any other online professional representation of you, and your personal brand.

LinkedIn Profile Picture:

Look at how beautiful I am!

Your perfect profile picture should tick the following boxes:

- Great lighting.

- Awesome resolution.
- A simple background.
- Full, glorious color.
- A neat, head and shoulders photograph of your face.

Long story short, you need a great picture. It seriously makes a world of difference. Don't ignore this.

Step 2: Write a summary statement that is accurate AND interesting.

Ok, now that I'm done yelling at you for having a bad photo, let's talk about your LinkedIn summary statement.

"Robbie is an innovative marketing professional with over 15 years of experience in the industry..."

Are you bored yet?

I am, and that sentence is all about me.

LinkedIn gives you 2,000 characters to provide a comprehensive window into who you are and what makes you tick, not just as an employee, but as a person. I mean, a 2,000 character-long bio on the internet is just a step below a full memoir. Am I right?

Your summary needs to sell you, but it needs to do it authentically.

Start at the beginning. Share your values. Have a sense of humor. Be a real, living, breathing person with goals, ambitions, fears, interests, skills, and hobbies. After reading your summary, your viewers should feel like they've just met you for a friendly chat over a cup of coffee.

Your summary should cover these 5 bases:

1) Value statement. This should be your very first sentence, and you better make it good. You don't have to focus on what you're currently doing: the point is to tell the reader exactly what they'd get out of working with you.

I help miserable people see the light in their career.

I help executives elevate their career through branding and recruiting.

2) Why I do what I do. Now that you've got their attention, use a couple of paragraphs to tell your story. Where have you been? What do you stand for? Use stories and anecdotes to keep things human and engaging.

Transitioning from IT to Digital Marketing & Career Advancement was one of the toughest transitions of my life.

I went through a life crisis trying to figure it all out. Going through a life and identity crisis while your bank account also depends on the answer is something I hope you never have to go through.

I went from being an expert in "IT Consulting" with 9 years experience to becoming a "Marketing Director" and "Career Advancement Expert" within 2 years.

I not only destroyed the ceiling that was preventing me from advancing, I positioned myself to never let a ceiling control my career and my life again. I've never felt this free in my entire life.

My goal is to help you learn from my mistakes.

3) Interesting facts. This is the main advantage of LinkedIn over a traditional resume: you can tell the reader anything you think they need to know. Perhaps you have expertise that isn't covered by your qualifications, or want to branch out in a direction where you have no formal experience. This is the place for things that don't fit under a bullet-point list.

INTERESTING FACTS

I wrote the book conservatively titled, "Fire Me I Beg You."

LinkedIn chose one of my posts as one of the best articles in 2014. My articles have accumulated over 3 million views with 4 posts over 400,000 views.

I built a strong professional network in Chicago with growing startups, investors, and successful entrepreneurs by taking 250 coffee meetings in 400 days.

The CEO of Deloitte Consulting loved my resignation letter so much that he sent it to the entire company. My writing has been featured in the New York Times, Business Insider, Forbes, CBS News, and Lifehacker.

I stalked James Altucher for 4 years. The result? He invited me to be a guest on his award winning podcast.

I built an email list of 10,000 people in 5 months using LinkedIn.

4) How I can help you. Time to lay it all on the line. This section isn't just about telling the reader what you can do, but emphasizes that you're willing to do it for them. You need to let them have the Holy Grail: give out your email address.

HOW CAN I HELP YOU?

If you think I can help you, please email me at robbie@firemeibegyou.com. I read every email.

I include the line: "Email me at robbie@firemeibegyou.com. I read every email."

That last little statement says two things: that you get a lot of emails, and that you make time for the people who send them to you.

5) Special skills. This section plays two parts. First, telling people what you do. Second, providing terms that will show up in keyword searches.

SKILLS

Digital Marketing, LinkedIn Coaching, Story Teller, Chicago Author, Chicago Speaker.

Step 3: Use the Media section.

This is why a LinkedIn profile pays 10 times more than a resume. Give some life to your profile and add anything interesting about you. Give them a reason to reach out to you.

Step 4: You need to fill in all of the fields, unfortunately.

This is a no-brainer, but it's an important one. And it doesn't mean just filling up each field with a stream-of-consciousness, buzzword-added nonsense will cut it.

Step 5: Fill out your job history. Include descriptions for each position in the first person!

Do not import your resume straight into LinkedIn. Yes, the option exists. But the option to buy and then eat thumbtacks also exists, and you don't need to be told not to do that. Do you?

Importing your resume forces your profile to be boring again. Focus on telling a great story instead of a bullet point story.

Also, does your experience at Wing Pit in college fit into the narrative as a Director of Marketing? You decide. But chances are, things like this can only hurt you.

Step 6: Ditch the buzzwords. You're not a motivated, team player. Trust me, no one believes you.

Truly innovative people don't say they're 'innovative' because they're too busy innovating.

Let your accomplishments do the talking for you, and try to avoid coming across like a repetitive corporate robot.

Hint: If the word synergy appears in your summary, it probably needs a rewrite.

Step 7: Stick to the first person.

Instead of saying, "Robbie is an experienced project management professional," you can say something along the lines of "I have worked in many Fortune 500 companies as a project manager. My specific focus is SAP software implementations."

If you're not used to blowing your own horn, it's time to sign up for trumpet lessons.

Using the third person makes it sound like you've got some kind of dissociative disorder, or that you're trying to make it sound like your profile summary came from someone else. The only items that should sound like they came from someone else are the glowing referrals on your profile.

Step 8: Think twice about any qualifications in your title.

I had my project management certification and the qualification was a "PMP". So I put my name as Robbie Abed, PMP. Long story short, I got more InMails from my friends that I'm missing the I in PMP, than I actually got from hiring managers.

I also realized that many hiring managers viewed a Project Management Certification as a nice to have, and not a must have.

Unless the job you want specifically requires that qualification (like a Medical Doctor), it's probably not that relevant to any recruiters looking to hire, and might actually pigeonhole you and limit your potential reach.

If you've got your diploma in journalism, but want to get into B2B communications, chances are that 'Dip.' abbreviation at the end of your name will make your profile views do just that.

Step 9: You might also want to reconsider naming the company you work for in your subtitle.

Similarly, if you're holding down a position at a well-known or particularly credible company, then you might do well to include the name in your title. But bear in mind that just saying 'Director of Sales' sounds more impressive than 'Director of Sales at Mrs. Tinsley's Instant Soup Factory'. Remember, dress for the job you want.

Step 10: You might even want to rethink your own name. Especially if your name is John Smith.

If your name is John Smith, you're screwed. You would literally have to find the cure to cancer, win an NFL championship and the Tour De France to even be considered for the first result for your name search on Google or LinkedIn.

If when you Google yourself you start realizing your name might not be as unique as you thought it was, it's time to start differentiating yourself. If you have a second name, or the option of a double-barrel surname, start adding that to your online profiles.

I'm not recommending you drop your last name, like Adele, Prince, or Rihanna. Nor do I think this is the ideal opportunity to use that great nickname you got in 5th grade.

'James Johnson' might not be memorable on its own, but add that second name your parents thoughtfully added to your birth certificate and now, Mr. James Peter Johnson, you've got a much better chance of being found online.

The key is to then use that same name across every online channel including your email signature.

Step 11: Your City – use this field strategically when looking for a job in a different city.

The 'city' field seems like an obvious one to get right. You just enter the city you're currently living and working in, right? Not so much. Let's say you're based in Fort Lauderdale, but have dreams of moving to New York.

You'd up and move if only the right career opportunity came along. But how is that opportunity going to come along when all of New York's hiring managers are striking you off their list because it looks like you're happy where you are. Correct their assumption.

List the city you want to work in to start getting noticed by recruiters in that area, so you can make sure you show up in their searches.

I'm not saying lie about your current location. Don't lie about where your current job is. Tell the truth, but you can put the city you want to work in and be Kosher in my book.

PART III

HOW TO BUILD NEW RELATIONSHIPS USING LINKEDIN

HOW TO BUILD NEW RELATIONSHIPS USING LINKEDIN

Three things you need to know about how to build great relationships using LinkedIn:

1. Build relationships before you need them.
2. Know exactly the types of people who can help you with your career or business in the future.
3. If your profile is not interesting, your response rates will diminish. Do I sound like a broken record yet?

Let's dive in to some tactics you can use to build new relationships.

Tactics to Build New Relationships

Scenario #1 - You read an article or post by someone who matches someone you want to connect with.

Step #1 - Comment on the post with an insightful comment.

Step #2 - Add them on LinkedIn with a custom note:

Example #1

Sean - I read your article on LinkedIn. I really liked your insight into project management. Would be great to stay connected so I can read more of your posts later. I'm also a PM. Thanks!

- Robbie

Example #2 - Coffee Request

Sean - I read your article on LinkedIn. I really liked your insight into project management. Would you be open to having coffee next Thursday? I'm always interested in meeting talented PM's in Chicago. I have nothing to sell you. Just looking to meet interesting people!

- Robbie

This connection request has a high probability of being accepted mainly because the person you are adding WANTS to be noticed. That's why he created content in the first place. See how that works? Is it all coming together now?

Scenario #2 - You found them on LinkedIn through search.

Pro-tip: The people that are most likely to accept your out-of-nowhere request usually have something in common with you, such as:

- Attended the same University
- Used to work at the same company as you
- Same or similar title
- Have mutual connections

So, the note when adding them should mention WHY you

want to connect with them and how you're similar to them. Here are some examples:

Example #1

Susanne - I also graduated from Purdue University. I love digital marketing and I'm looking to connect with other successful marketers from Purdue. It would be great to connect and potentially work together in the future.

P.S. It's great that you worked at Microsoft. It's a great company. Boiler up!

- Robbie

Example #2

Susanne - I used to work at Accenture after I graduated college as well. I was in the Systems Integration department. I don't believe we've met, but you have a similar career path as me. It would be great to connect and learn from each other via LinkedIn.

Thank You!

- Robbie

Example #3

Susanne - I have 3 mutual connections with you. I ran across your profile and really enjoyed your article about the future of technology. It's amazing what has happened in such a short time.

I would love to connect with you and hopefully we can learn from each other!

Thank You!

- Robbie

Convert offline relationships to online relationships

I think the most underused feature of LinkedIn is figuring out how to maintain relationships.

LinkedIn is the center of your career. If you want others to be aware of what you're working on, then you must be diligent about adding new connections on LinkedIn.

Met someone at a networking event and spoke with them for more than 90 seconds?

Add them on LinkedIn.

Met a friend of a friend and you only spoke to them on the phone?

Add them on LinkedIn.

Interacted with someone on twitter that you want to build a better relationship with?

Follow them on Twitter. Add them on LinkedIn.

See where I'm going with this?

"Hi, I'd like to add you to my professional network on LinkedIn."

God might accept your request too!

The beautiful part about LinkedIn is that it's not creepy to ask someone to get connected. Adding someone on Facebook after only speaking to them for 90 seconds is kind of creepy if you ask me. But on LinkedIn, it's acceptable.

How to Handle Random LinkedIn Connections

Should you accept random connections?

There are two ways to answer this question:

1) No way. Protect your network. Keep it as intimate as possible.

2) Yes way. Every connection is one more person that can spread your message far and wide.

NO WAY:

Pros:

1. Everyone on your network is someone you can vouch for.
2. Your news feed is nicely curated and has relevant content from your connections.

Cons:

1. The reach for your content is limited.
2. You restrict the ability to make new connections and potentially limit a number of opportunities.

YES WAY:

Pros:

1. The potential reach for your content is multiplied. This can increase your opportunities and social proof.

Cons:

1. Your news feed becomes useless since it's filled with topics from random strangers who you'll never meet.
2. You'll miss out on closer connections' announcements and contacts.

THE MIDDLE GROUND WAY:

Respond back to the request and ask them if you know them from somewhere and why they reached out to connect. I usually say, "Hi, Stacy - Thanks for connecting. Have we met before? Is there a particular reason you reached out to me? Thanks again! Looking forward to connecting with you."

There is no wrong answer in my opinion. Choose wisely, my friend.

How Long Does it Take to Build a Relationship?

I am not a patient person.

If someone is fumbling to pay in the grocery line, I get frustrated. If the pause between someone saying, "Hey, Robbie!" and the next words that come out of their mouth is too long, I get frustrated. I'll make myself a sandwich and eat it in the kitchen before sitting down. I don't have time to sit down and enjoy it.

But when it comes to relationships, I play the long game.

I haven't used any statistics this entire book, so I'm not about to drop one now. All I know is that if your plan is to build relationships, don't expect immediate results. Relationships take time. A long time.

How do I speed up the time it takes to build a relationship?

I knew you wouldn't listen to me. I knew you didn't want to hear that it takes a long time.

Here's the deal. I'll tell you how to cut the time in half.

Think of two people you've never met before, but you would trust to do business with.

What do those two individuals have in common? Without knowing who you picked, I know what they have in common.

Respect.

You respect them. You appreciate what they've achieved. You recognize the amount of time they've put into their craft. You admire their ability to teach others and give back to the community.

So, how do you speed up the time to build a relationship?

Do something that earns the respect of your connections.

The more you use LinkedIn as a teaching platform, the faster your connections will trust you. Knowing, liking, and trusting are the three things needed to build a flourishing relationship. No word-for-word script will tell you how to do that.

PART IV

HOW TO GET JOB OFFERS

HOW TO GET JOB OFFERS

This is how 99% of people search for jobs today:

THIS WAY SUCKS:

1. See job application.
2. Apply for it online.
3. Yell at your computer for having to fill out 100 fields.
4. Wish for the best.
5. Don't hear anything back.
6. Depression.
7. Repeat Steps 1-6.

THIS WAY IS BETTER:

1. See job application.
2. Find out how you're connected to the company.
3. Reach out.
4. Get referred directly to the hiring manager.
5. Interview.

6. Job offer.
7. Happiness!
8. Repeat steps 1-7.

This diagram accurately describes how the job search should be.

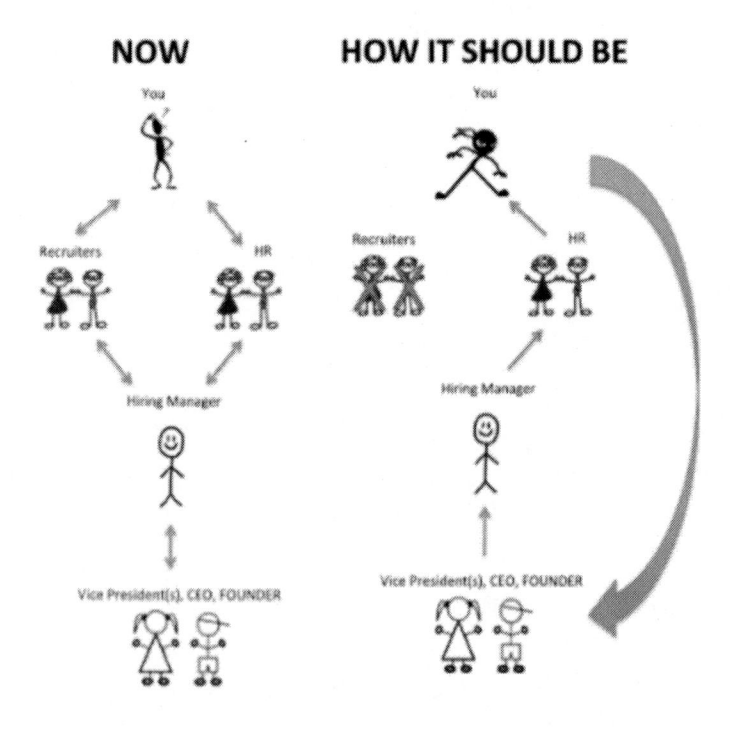

NOW — You, Recruiters, HR, Hiring Manager, Vice President(s), CEO, FOUNDER

HOW IT SHOULD BE — You, Recruiters, HR, Hiring Manager, Vice President(s), CEO, FOUNDER

The fastest and easiest way to getting a new job or building a new business relationship is through a referral.

This often helps you "get around the system." The less gatekeepers you have to go through, the better off you are.

I know this news isn't going to surprise you. **Employers**

prefer candidates who get referred from within the company as opposed to applying online.

In other words: No Shit Sherlock.

But I'm still not convinced you totally understand how big referrals are. Here is a great quote from a NY Times Article:

"Even getting in the door for an interview is becoming more difficult for those without connections. Referred candidates are twice as likely to land an interview as other applicants, according to a new study of one large company by three economists from the Federal Reserve Bank of New York. For those who make it to the interview stage, the referred candidates had a 40 percent better chance of being hired than other applicants."

A 40% better chance!

Human resource departments have recognized the same pattern. "Our analysis shows referred hires perform better, stay longer and are quicker to integrate into our teams," said Mr. Nash of Ernst & Young.

As a result, within the last two years, firms like Deloitte, Ernst & Young, and Booz Allen have created dedicated teams within their human resource departments to shepherd prospects through the system. Over all, Deloitte receives more than 400,000 résumés a year, but recommended employees are guided along by a 12-person team.

Robbie, Robbie. We get it. How do we maximize referrals?

Easy, tiger. I'm going to get there.

No, seriously, Robbie. How do I maximize referrals on LinkedIn? Don't mess with me.

Fine. Let's have an honest conversation about getting new jobs and new business using referrals.

Let's dispel some myths right away:

It's NOT who you know. A large network doesn't guarantee success. I have seen a lot of people who know everyone and their mother's brother's cousin and still struggle to find a job.

It's who you know that knows EXACTLY what you do.

Let's take it one step further.

The more people that:

- Know who you are.
- Know EXACTLY what you do.
- Are confident that you would do an amazing job (social proof, anyone?).

The higher the chance you will be referred.

Referrals are your path to success. Everything else is playing the game on hard mode.

How to Go From a Job Posting to a Conversation With a VP or Hiring Manager Using a Referral:

Scenario: You see a job posting online you think you're qualified for.

The Plan: Go around the system. Get a direct connection to the hiring manager or VP of the department.

Step 1. Don't apply for it. Seriously, don't apply for it. This is the LAST step if all else fails.

Step 2. Look up the company name on LinkedIn.

Step 3. Take a best guess on who the hiring manager is for that position, or find the VP who oversees that department. It's important to have a hit list. Don't look at who HR is unless you're applying for an HR role. LinkedIn makes this easy. When you're on the company profile page, it will show you how many connections you have at that company.

Usually what I will do is click on the "See all 141,796 employees on LinkedIn" link and find attributes of someone who I think will oversee that job posting.

17 connections work here.
See all 141,796 employees on LinkedIn →

Step 4. See if you have any mutual connections with ANYONE who works at that company.

Let's say that I'm looking to work for Microsoft in their marketing department.

After clicking on the link from Step 2, I then filter my results.

I will find all of my first and second-degree connections that work at Microsoft and have the title "Marketing Director." This will help me find the relevant Marketing VP's who I'm connected with or I have a close connection with.

3rd degree is usually harder to navigate, so I just ignore it.

Filter people by   Clear all (4)

Connections ^

☑ 1st   ☑ 2nd   ☐ 3rd+

Keywords ^

First name

[   ]

Last name

[   ]

Title

[Marketing Director   ]

Company

[   ]

School

[   ]

Locations ⌄

Current companies ^

☑ Microsoft

Here are the results that come up:

Matthew Kresch · 2nd
Director of Product Marketing, Microsoft Dynamics
Greater Seattle Area

Current: Director of Product Marketing, Microsoft Dynamics

(5 shared connections)

Heather Deggans · 2nd
Sr. Director of US Field Marketing (Enterprise, Corpo
Greater Seattle Area

(2 shared connections)

Debbie Hutchings · 2nd
Director, Marketing, Cloud + Enterprise at Microsoft
Greater Seattle Area

Current: Director, Marketing, Cloud + Enterprise at Microsoft

(3 shared connections)

Great! I have a lot of common connections to these Directors. NOW, here's where the moment of truth comes.

Do those shared connections know how good you are at what you do?

Have you been following Robbie's advice to post original content on LinkedIn?

I know you haven't spoken to them in a while, but if you

posted great content consistently, they would definitely notice!

DO YOU SEE WHERE I'M GOING WITH THIS?????

DO YOU SEE HOW IT ALL BUILDS UP TO THIS ONE MOMENT?????

Ok. No more caps lock.

You get the point.

I'm going to cover what you can write to these connections anyway, but understand when I tell you, it's not about what you write.

It's about who you represent. The better you represent yourself on LinkedIn, the easier it becomes.

Step 4a. You have a 1st degree connection with someone who works at the company? Reach out to them via inMail or email and say:

Hi, John - I saw a job posted online for the company you currently work for. Here's the link. Do you know anything about the position? Do you know the best way to learn more about this position? I would love to speak to someone internally before I apply.

P.S. How's life? Did you ever finish writing that book?

Thanks!

OR

Hi, John - How well do you know Stacy Smith, VP of Digital?

I saw a job posted online at Acme Corp and I wanted to

learn more about it. Do you know Stacy Smith well? I would really like to speak with her about the position before I apply.

Any recommendations on the best way to approach this? You COULD have an awesome teammate :)

P.S. How's life? Run any marathons lately?

Thank You!

Step 4b. You don't know anyone who works at the company, but you know someone who knows someone who does work at that company (AKA, 2nd degree connection).

Hi, John - How well do you know Stacy Smith, VP of Digital at Acme X?

I saw a job posted online for Acme X and I think Stacy Smith would be the hiring manager. Do you know her well? With her permission, would you be able to connect us?

P.S. How's life? I saw your poster at the burger joint for eating 100 double cheeseburgers in one sitting. That's amazing!

Thanks!

Robbie

Step 4c. You don't have any 1st or 2nd degree connections.

Reach out to the hiring manager directly.

Hi, John - Coffee?

John - I saw the digital marketing lead job posted on LinkedIn. Before I applied, I wanted to speak with someone from your team and ask a few questions. There are a few areas where I can help your company grow, but wanted to understand the role a little bit more.

Are you free next Tuesday or Wednesday?

My LinkedIn profile has all my credentials. Thank You!

Step 5. No reply? Apply for the job online.

But, I would make sure you exhausted every possibility to get connected or referred to the company before applying.

Step 6. Have an out-of-body experience and re-evaluate your LinkedIn profile. You need to be 7/7 interesting.

LinkedIn will never replace face-to-face conversations.

I don't care how good you are at LinkedIn or digital marketing, nothing replaces face-to-face conversations.

LinkedIn should be used for keeping in touch with people and establishing your authority as someone who knows what they are talking about.

An in-person meeting is where the opportunity really happens.

You need a healthy mix.

If you feel you haven't seen society in a while, it's a good idea to reach out to a few people for coffee and catch up with them.

PART V

HOW TO GET NOTICED ON LINKEDIN

HOW TO GET NOTICED ON LINKEDIN

Getting noticed isn't about going viral.

It's about the right people seeing the right message over and over.

So, if you don't have similar results to what I have, please don't fret.

You're not supposed to attract thousands of people to your profile.

I'm a career advancement author who also happens to be a marketer. EVERYONE on LinkedIn is my audience!

You and I most likely don't have the same audience.

So, if you're looking to go viral on LinkedIn, you're reading the next few chapters for the wrong reason.

There are really two ways to get noticed on LinkedIn:

1) Short form posts, which I will call "Status Messages" for the rest of this book.

2) Long form posts, also known as "LinkedIn Publisher."

Status Messages: Drive your message home every day.

There's a great question on Babycenter.com:

Why does my child insist on watching the same videos over and over?

"Young children love repetition, whether it's watching a video or listening to song lyrics, because it's the best way for them to acquire and master new skills. In order to learn something well, children this age practice it until they get it right, hence the repeated watching.

What is your child practicing by repeatedly watching a video? It depends on the video, of course, but it could be that he doesn't yet understand the story line. And the more he watches, the better he's able to understand.

Maybe he's fascinated by programs that feature songs and dancing and wants to practice the movements while singing along. Young children are almost always in the process of mastering basic skills while they play.

Once your child has mastered a video's dialog or song lyrics or movements, he wants to celebrate his success by participating in what he's seeing, so he'll continue to watch.

He'll probably announce the next plot sequence or song (in his head or out loud); for children this age, making correct predictions is the ultimate form of mastery. Since life is fairly unpredictable for them, they especially relish feeling competent and in control of what's coming next."

Adults are no different from children. We want to learn. We NEED to hear the same message over and over.

So, if you feel that you have to "mix it up" with different messages you post on LinkedIn, then you're not thinking straight. Find a message that works and don't be afraid to keep repeating it. It's the only way to get noticed.

Please don't take this to mean you should copy and paste your status messages every other day.

Post a different perspective, but keep the messaging inline.

Here are some examples that a project manager can post on LinkedIn:

DAY 1:

Project management is all about communication. The most successful projects that I've led as a project manager have been because the technical and functional teams were transparent with me when it came to reporting status.

DAY 3:

If your team is going to miss a deadline for a project and

you're the PM, it's best practice that you not only let the team know they're behind, but work with them individually to understand how you can help prevent this in the future.

Stop yourself from blaming others for the delays. Go by each person's desk and ask how you can help. Do they need other teams to finish their deliverables earlier? Do they need to stop getting random requests that take up their time? Figure out the issue and provide a path forward. That's what a good PM will do.

DAY 5:

I personally don't think the project manager software matters much. I've worked with every PM software and it always came down to in-person communication the most.

I realized early in my career as a project manager that communication is always #1. The best software will help you focus on critical communication and not the little details.

This can go on for an entire year.

PRO-TIP: The more comments and likes a post gets, the farther it will spread. The best approach to maximizing reach is to post a message with a question at the end. This will help you get more comments and you will see your post spread because of it.

Your followers WILL notice it. They might not see every message, but after the 10th message, they will for sure know you're a project manager and have a passion for your craft.

When an opportunity comes up on their team and they

need a project manager, do you know who they will think of?

The man who posts stupid motivational quotes? Or the woman who posted useful information about project management every other day for the past 6 months?

THAT'S how you get noticed.

Consistency is power.

Again, the days of getting that many views are much harder. But the two common traits of those articles are that they are focused on personal stories with lessons learned.

I didn't just jump into a top ten list of random things. It was from experience. This also worked for me because I was working on positioning myself as a career expert.

Publishing Platform: It's All About the Story.

I built a big audience using the publishing platform. This is during the good ole days of LinkedIn where they would feature long form articles on the top of the home page.

Even though they don't feature the posts like they used to, this is still a great way to get noticed. The formula for getting noticed, however, still hasn't changed.

A good personal story with a single lesson learned always wins.

The two that come to mind are the two articles below. They have 429,000 and 543,000 views, respectively!

The Biggest Career Killer of All Time: The Performance Review
Robbie Abed on LinkedIn
October 28, 2014

✎ Edit   🗑 Delete   📈 **429,753 clicks** of your article

This was an article I posted recently. 3,427 views isn't 347,000 views but from my viewpoint, it was a success. I received a LOT of messages because of this post.

How to Get the Job Every Single Time -- Interviewing Techniques That Work
Robbie Abed on LinkedIn
May 4, 2017

✏ Edit   🗑 Delete   📈 3,427 clicks of your article

Again, I was focused on my personal experiences and what I know.

You'll notice that I don't write articles about how to manage a team. I know how to manage a team, but I honestly don't care enough to write about it.

The same concept applies for publishing platform as it does for posting status messages. Keep a consistent message.

You can't expect your connections to read everything you write, but they will see it in their feed. The more you keep the messaging inline, the more you will implant in their brain that you're good at what you do.

You're 7/7, good!

You're Not Selling Ice Cold Lemonade in 100 Degree Weather - Don't Expect Immediate Results.

I challenged myself to create a YouTube video every day for a month. I called it "Coffee with Robbie."

Every morning, I went to my office and the first thing I did was create a video of me giving career advice. As soon as I was finished, I uploaded it to YouTube and shared it on Facebook. No editing allowed since that would take forever.

Here's what happened.

1st video - 50+ likes, tons of comments.

2nd video - 30 likes, some comments.

3rd video - 10 likes, fewer comments.

4th video - 5 likes, 1 or 2 comments.

5th video to 12th video - A few likes and comments.

13th video - I start getting emails from old colleagues. They are wondering what I'm doing and want to learn more.

20th video - I start getting emails from strangers asking me if I can help them. Old colleagues that I'm friends with on Facebook are now referring me to their friends.

21st video - Coffee with Robbie is the center conversation at my family's Thanksgiving dinner.

Here's the deal: **Consistency will get you noticed even if your engagement is low.**

If you're consistently posting valuable status messages and articles on LinkedIn, YOU WILL GET NOTICED.

The flow looks like this: Who's Robbie? -> What is Robbie doing? -> What does Robbie do again? -> He seems interesting, I would like to meet him. -> I would like to work with him one day. He knows what he's talking about.

Consistency is the hardest, but most effective marketing strategy of all time.

In Conclusion

Imagine someone created a database of every professional in the world and provided you the ability to reach any of them with a click of a button and some text.

Someone already created it.

It's called LinkedIn.

There is only one reason that someone joins LinkedIn.

To build relationships, get noticed, and get job offers.

It's the same reason you're reading this book.

Use this knowledge to your advantage.

About Robbie

I'm an author, ghostwriter, and marketer. I'm also a contributing writer for Inc. Magazine. I started my career as an IT Consultant at Accenture & Deloitte. That's where I learned how to be a professional.

I quit consulting to become Director of IT for a mid-size company. It was the worst job of my life, so I quit and eventually wrote "Fire Me I Beg You" which was inspired by this job.

Apparently, if you want to write a book, you also have to market it. That's how I got into the marketing world. I also helped a few companies grow through marketing, and now I'm focused on writing and career development.

I learn something new every day. Once I get to a point where I believe I mastered a topic, I'll write about it.

Thank you for reading.

Robbie Abed

Hire Robbie

There are three reasons you would hire Robbie:

#1 - You want to write content, but you hate writing, and you don't have the bandwidth to write.

I'm a ghostwriter and can help you create content that will impact your career in a big way.

Email me at robbie@firemeibegyou.com with the subject line: "Ghost"

#2 - You're a miserable human being and are struggling with your career.

Most of my content is free, and I recommend starting there. I would go to my blog first (http://firemeibegyou.com), and sign up for the "Summer of Quitting" program.

If that doesn't work, email me at robbie@firemeibegyou.com with the subject line "Miserable"

#3 - Your sales or recruiting team needs help with LinkedIn.

I'll be more than happy to do a half-day or full-day workshop.

Email me at robbie@firemeibegyou.com with the subject line: "Training"